Dinosaur Dinners

Written

DK | Penguin Random House

Series Editor Deborah Lock
Senior Editors Shannon Beatty, Linda Esposito
Project Editors Mary Atkinson, Caryn Jenner
Editors Regina Kahney, Arpita Nath
Art Editors Karen Lieberman, Tanvi Nathyal
Senior Art Editor Ann Cannings
Picture Researchers Aditya Katyal, Mary Sweeney
Producer, Pre-production Marc Staples
Senior Producer, Pre-production Francesca Wardell
DTP Designers Sachin Singh, Anita Yadav
Jacket Designers Natalie Godwin, Charlotte Jennings
Managing Editor Soma B. Chowdhury
Deputy Managing Art Editor Jane Horne
Managing Art Editor Ahlawat Gunjan
Art Director Martin Wilson
Scientific Consultant Dr. Angela Milner

Reading Consultant
Linda Gambrell, Ph.D.

First American Edition, 1998
Other editions, 2011
This edition, 2015

Published in the United States by
DK Publishing
345 Hudson Street,
New York, New York 10014

Copyright © 1998, 2015 Dorling Kindersley Limited
DK, a Division of Penguin Random House LLC

15 16 17 18 19 10 9 8 7 6 5 4 3 2 1
001-271723-September/15

A catalog record for this book is available from the Library of Congress.

ISBN: 978-1-4654-3492-0 (Paperback)
ISBN: 978-1-4654-3493-7 (Hardback)

DK books are available at special discounts when purchased in bulk for sales promotions,
premiums, fund-raising, or educational use. For details, contact:
DK Publishing Special Markets
345 Hudson Street, New York, New York 10014
SpecialSales@dk.com

Printed and bound in China.

The publisher would like to thank the following:
(Key: a=above, b=below/bottom, c=center, l=left, r=right, t=top)
3 Fotolia: DM7
Museums: Natural History Museum, London, and Royal Tyrrel Museum of Palaeontolgy, Alberta.
Artists/model makers: Roby Braun, Jim Channell, Russell Gooday, John Holmes, Jon Hughes,
Graham High / Jeremy Hunt / Centaur Studios, Andrew Kerr, Gary Kevin, Kenneth Lilly, and Peter Minister
Photographers: Andy Crawford, John Downs, Neil Fletcher, Dave King, Tim Ridley, and Dave Rudkin.
Jacket images: Front: Dorling Kindersley: Jon Hughes. Getty Images: parema / E+ bc. **Back:** Dorling Kindersley:
John Holmes - modelmaker / Natural History Museum, London c.

All other images © Dorling Kindersley
For further information see: www.dkimages.com

A WORLD OF IDEAS:
SEE ALL THERE IS TO KNOW

www.dk.com

Contents

See the Dinosaur Glossary for a guide
to pronouncing dinosaur names.

What Did Dinosaurs Eat?

Different dinosaurs ate different kinds of food.

Meat Eaters

Dinosaurs that ate only meat are called **carnivores**.

Tyrannosaurus

I eat meat.

Plant Eaters

Dinosaurs that ate only plants are called **herbivores**.

Styracosaurus

I eat plants.

I eat both meat and plants.

Meat and Plant Eaters

Dinosaurs that ate both meat and plants are called **omnivores**.

Gallimimus

I am a dinosaur
looking for my breakfast.

I can see you,
wherever you are.

Troodon

I am a dinosaur
ready for my lunch.

Herrerasaurus

I can catch you,
even if you run.

I am a dinosaur,
hungry for my dinner.
I am bigger than you are.

Tyrannosaurus

11

We all have
sharp teeth and claws.
We are meat eaters.
We eat other dinosaurs.

Tyrannosaurus

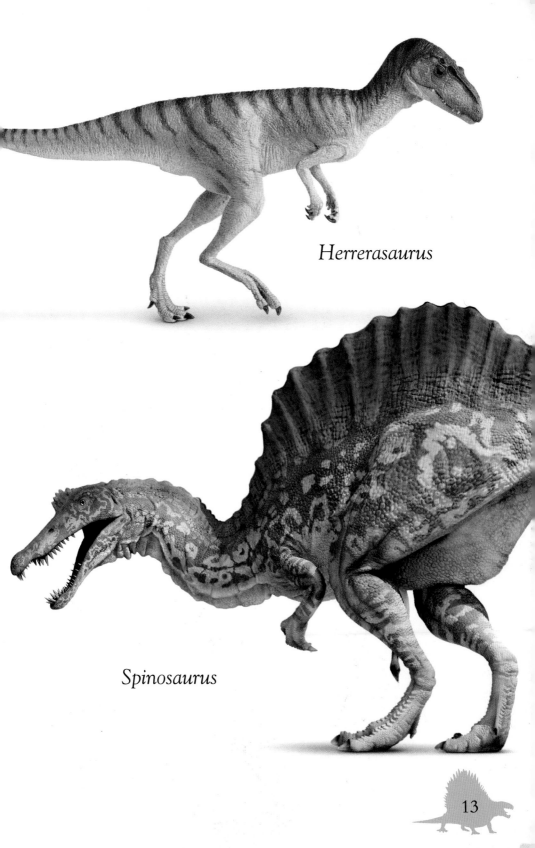

Herrerasaurus

Spinosaurus

13

Meat Eaters

Meat eaters ate fish, insects, small mammals, reptiles, and other dinosaurs.

Tyrannosaurus

Size: 37 feet long (12 meters)
Features: sharp teeth to tear meat and crush bones
Food: large dinosaurs

Troodon

Size: 6 feet long (2 meters)
Features: large eyes
for spotting prey
Food: small animals

Spinosaurus

Size: 52 feet long (16 meters)
Features: powerful jaw
Food: fish and dinosaurs

15

Plant Eaters

Most dinosaurs were plant eaters. They had to watch out for meat eaters who wanted to eat them!

Barosaurus
This slow-moving dinosaur fed on all kinds of plants.

Edmontonia
This dinosaur's low-set head made it easier to eat grass.

Plateosaurus
This dinosaur stood on strong hind legs to eat leaves.

Brachiosaurus
This "gentle giant" used its long neck to reach high trees.

17

I am a dinosaur
who only eats plants.
I stay close to my babies
to protect them from meat eaters.

Maiasaura

I made their nest
from a mound of earth.
I bring leaves and berries
for them to eat.

We are small but fast.
We eat plants that
grow close to the ground.

Hypsilophodon

We live in a herd.
If one of us spots a meat eater,
we all zoom off
on our strong back legs.

I look frightening
because I am so big.

I need to eat
huge amounts of leaves
to keep myself going.
I use my long neck
to reach the leaves
at the tops of trees.

Barosaurus

I can see danger coming
from any direction.
I am much taller than
any of the meat eaters.

Dinosaurs that don't eat meat
need protection from those that do.
Our spikes are long and sharp.
If meat eaters come too close,
we take them on head first.

Styracosaurus

25

DINOSAUR BATTLE

Plant eaters had to defend themselves from meat eaters.

Lesothosaurus

- Plant eater
- Big eyes for all-around view
- Lightweight and speedy

Coelophysis

- Meat eater
- Long neck, sharp claws
- More than 100 sharp, curved teeth

WHO WILL WIN?

Sharp teeth cannot dent
my body armor.
And watch out for the spikes
on my shoulders.
One bump from me
and it's the end.

Edmontonia

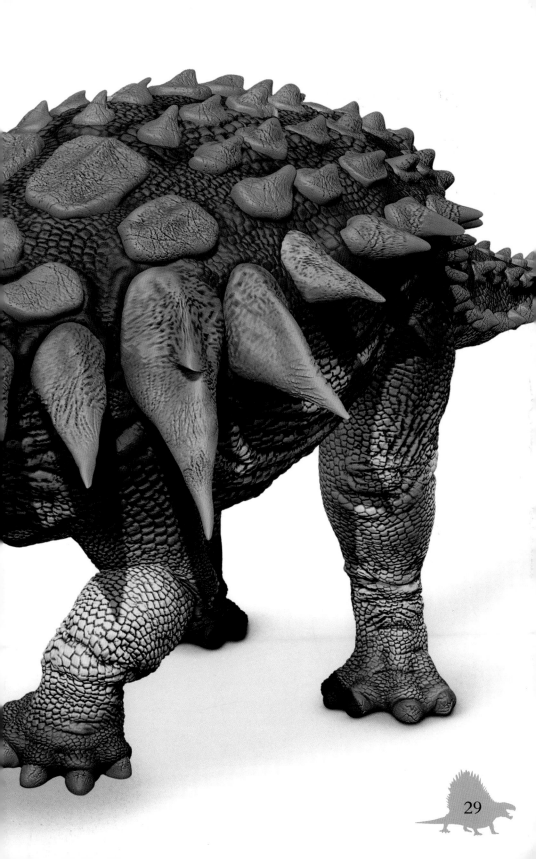

29

My skin is as hard as a rock.
My body is covered
in studs, spikes, and horns.

I swing the club
on the end of my tail.
It can break the legs
of the bigger dinosaurs.

I am not very big,
but I am dangerous.

Euoplocephalus

We don't need special weapons.
If we smell danger,
we raise the alarm.
We use our head crests like trumpets
to make loud hooting calls.

Parasaurolophus

Corythosaurus

33

We are all dinosaurs that eat plants.
We all have some way
of protecting ourselves
from meat eaters.

Styracosaurus

Barosaurus

Euoplocephalus

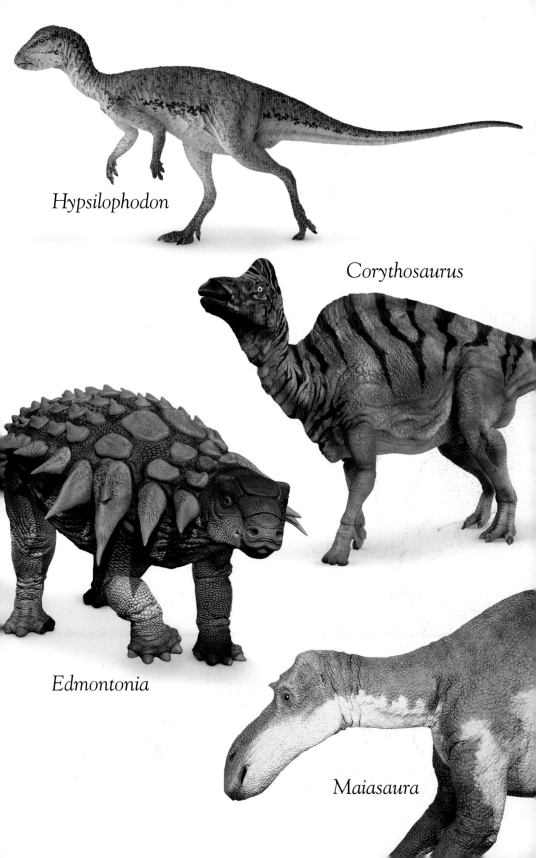

Hypsilophodon

Corythosaurus

Edmontonia

Maiasaura

Eat or be eaten?
That is the dinosaur question.

I can run fast enough to get away
from the big meat eaters.
I can also run fast enough
to catch small animals.

Gallimimus

I like to eat lizards
and other animals.
I catch them with
my strong claws
and my long beak.
But I eat plants, too.
I am not a picky eater.

Dinosaur Game

You will need a counter for each player and a die. Players take turns to throw the die and move their counters.

START

It's a hungry Herrerasaurus. MOVE BACK 1 SPACE.

A Barosaurus eats lots of plants to clear the path for you. MOVE FORWARD 1 SPACE.

FINISH

Watch a Maiasaura mom feed her babies.
MISS A TURN.

A Gallimimus chases you.
MOVE FORWARD 2 SPACES.

A hooting Corythosaurus warns you of danger.
MOVE BACK 1 SPACE.

A Styracosaurus defends you.
MOVE FORWARD 1 SPACE.

We are all dinosaurs.
What do we eat for dinner?

Who Am I?

Match the dinosaurs to the clues.

Gallimimus

Barosaurus

Tyrannosaurus

Euoplocephalus

1. I use my tail club to protect myself from meat eaters.

2. I run very fast. I hunt small reptiles, such as lizards.

3. I am one of the biggest meat-eating dinosaurs.

4. I have a long neck to reach the leaves at the tops of trees.

5. I eat both plants and animals!

Herrerasaurus

1. Euoplocephalus;
2. Herrerasaurus; 3. Tyrannosaurus;
4. Barosaurus; 5. Gallimimus.

43

Dinosaur Glossary

Barosaurus
(BAR-oh-sore-us)
• name means "heavy lizard"
• herbivore

Brachiosaurus
(BRAK-ee-oh-sore-us)
• name means "arm lizard"
• herbivore

Coelophysis
(seel-OH-fie-sis)
• name means "hollow form"
• carnivore

Corythosaurus
(koh-rith-OH-sore-us)
• name means "helmet lizard"
• herbivore

Edmontonia
(ed-mon-TONE-ee-ah)
• name means "from Edmonton"
  (Canada)
• herbivore

Euoplocephalus
(you-OH-plo-kef-ah-luss)
• name means "well-armored head"
• herbivore

Gallimimus
(gal-lee-MEEM-us)
• name means "chicken mimic"
• omnivore

Herrerasaurus
(herr-ray-rah-SORE-us)
• name means "Herrera's lizard"
  after Victorino Herrera who
  discovered it
• carnivore

Hypsilophodon
(hip-sih-LOH-foh-don)
• name means "high ridge tooth"
• herbivore

Lesothosaurus
(Le-SO-toe-sore-us)
• name means "Lizard from
  Lesotho (Africa)"
• herbivore

Maiasaura
(my-ah-SORE-ah)
• name means "good mother lizard"
• herbivore

Parasaurolophus
(pa-ra-saw-ROL-off-us)
• name means "beside ridge lizard"
• herbivore

Plateosaurus
(plat-ee-oh-sore-us)
• name means "flat lizard"
• herbivore

Spinosaurus
(SPINE-oh-SORE-us)
• name means "thorn lizard"
• carnivore

Styracosaurus
(sty-RAK-oh-sore-us)
• name means "spiked lizard"
• herbivore

Troodon
(TROH-oh-don)
• name means "wounding tooth"
• carnivore

Tyrannosaurus
(tie-RAN-oh-sore-us)
• name means "tyrant lizard"
• carnivore

Index

Guide for Parents

DK Readers is a four-level interactive reading adventure series for children, developing the habit of reading widely for both pleasure and information. These books have an exciting main narrative interspersed with a range of reading genres to suit your child's reading ability, as required by the Common Core State Standards. Each book is designed to develop your child's reading skills, fluency, grammar awareness, and comprehension in order to build confidence and engagement when reading.

Ready for a *Beginning to Read Alone* book

YOUR CHILD SHOULD

- be able to read many words without needing to stop and break them down into sound parts.
- read smoothly, in phrases and with expression.
  By this level, your child will be beginning to read silently.
- self-correct when a word or sentence doesn't sound right.

A VALUABLE AND SHARED READING EXPERIENCE

For some children, text reading, particularly nonfiction, requires much effort, but adult participation can make this both fun and easier. So here are a few tips on how to use this book with your child.

TIP 1 Check out the contents together before your child begins:
- invite your child to check the blurb, contents page, and layout of the book and comment on it.
- ask your child to make predictions about the story.
- talk about the information your child might want to find out.

TIP 2 Encourage fluent and flexible reading:
- support your child to read in fluent, expressive phrases, making full use of punctuation and thinking about the meaning.

- help your child learn to read with expression by choosing a sentence to read aloud and demonstrating how to do this.

TIP 3 Indicators that your child is reading for meaning:

- your child will be responding to the text if he/she is self-correcting and varying his/her voice.
- your child will want to talk about what he/she is reading or is eager to turn the page to find out what will happen next.

TIP 4 Chat at the end of each chapter:

- encourage your child to recall specific details after each chapter.
- let your child pick out interesting words and discuss what they mean.
- talk about what each of you found most interesting or most important.
- ask questions about the text. These help to develop comprehension skills and awareness of the language used.

A FEW ADDITIONAL TIPS

- Read to your child regularly to demonstrate fluency, phrasing, and expression; to find out or check information; and for sharing enjoyment.
- Encourage your child to reread favorite texts to increase reading confidence and fluency.
- Check that your child is reading a range of different types of material, such as poems, jokes, and following instructions.

Series consultant, **Dr. Linda Gambrell**, Distinguished Professor of Education at Clemson University, has served as President of the National Reading Conference, the College Reading Association, and the International Reading Association. She is also reading consultant for the **DK Adventures**.

Have you read these other great books from DK?

BEGINNING TO READ ALONE ②

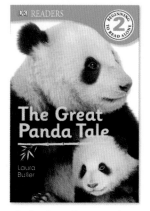

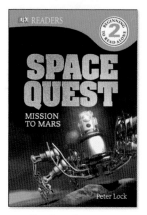

What spits out fire and ash or explodes with a bang? Volcanoes!

Join Louise at the zoo, helping to welcome a new panda baby.

Embark on a mission to explore the solar system. First stop—Mars.

READING ALONE ③

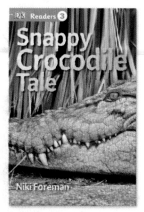

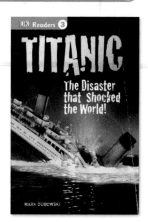

Follow Chris Croc's adventures in Australia from a baby to a mighty king of the river.

Design and test a rocket for a flying mission. Try out some experiments at home.

This is the incredible true story of the "unsinkable" ship that sank.